PAPER TRICKS II

by Florence Temko

Drawings by Sandra Dennis

SCHOLASTIC INC.
New York Toronto London Auckland Sydney

HELPFUL HINTS

WHEN YOU SEE THIS:	IT MEANS:

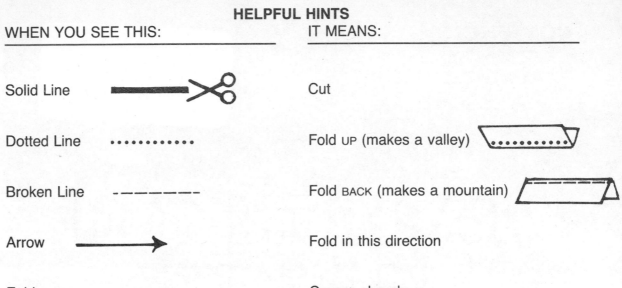

Solid Line — Cut

Dotted Line — Fold UP (makes a valley)

Broken Line — Fold BACK (makes a mountain)

Arrow — Fold in this direction

Fold — Crease sharply

Read all the way through the instructions before you begin a project. If you want to make more than one copy of any of the projects, trace the pattern on another piece of paper before you cut it out.

ISBN 0-590-43333-4

Copyright © 1990 by Florence Temko. All rights reserved. Published by Scholastic Inc.

12 11 10 9 8

Printed in the U.S.A.

First Scholastic printing, September 1990

CONTENTS

Flying French Fries, 5

Amazing Coin Trick, 7

Howling Coyote, 9

Santa Claus, 11

Mystery of the Paper Clips, 13

Earrings, 15

Windsurfer's Race, 17

Jumping Mice, 19

Pop-up Valentine, 21

Hi-flying Airplane, 23

The Broken Plate Puzzle, 25

Heavenly Angel, 27

Droopy Dog, 29

Starry Nights, 31

Beautiful Butterflies, 35

Space Shuttle, 37

Nine-Makes-Ten Trick, 39

Fighting Turtles Game, 41

Origami Holiday Ornament, 43

Winged Dinosaur, 45

FLYING
FRENCH FRIES

. Cut out the Flying
French Fries on all
the solid lines.
. Fold up on dotted
lines 1 and 2.
. Fold on dotted lines
3 and 4, overlapping
the paper.
. Fold one French Fry
to you on line 5.

5. Fold the other
French Fry away
from you on line 6.
6. Put a paper clip on
the bottom. Raise
the flyer over your
head and drop it
gently. Watch it twirl
down.
See back of page.

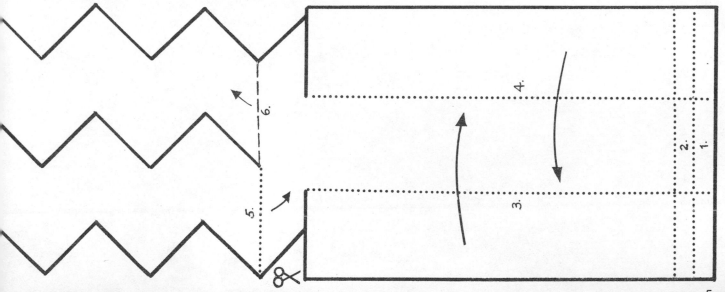

Suggestion

Decorations: Color th
wings yellow and
brown.

AMAZING COIN TRICK

This is an easy trick you can play on your friends. They cannot push a quarter through the small hole shown in the middle of the page. But *you* can do it! Here is how you prepare the trick:

1. Cut out the square on the solid lines.
2. Poke the point of the scissors into the middle of the circle. Carefully cut out the circle exactly on the line.
3. Show the paper and a quarter to your friends. Challenge anyone to push the quarter through the hole, without tearing the paper. Nobody can do it!

See back of page for the solution.

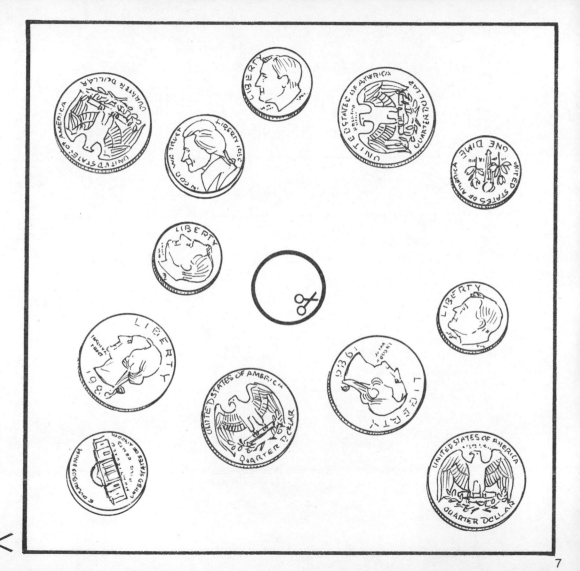

Solution for the coin trick:

Fold the paper in half and place the quarter inside. Hold the paper on the side as shown. Push your hands toward each other and the top edges come apart in the middle. Now the quarter goes through.

HOWLING COYOTE

Cut out the square.
Fold to the BACK on
the broken line.
Cut out the coyote
through both layers
of paper.
Unfold the paper flat.
The coyote stands
up.
Color the coyote any
way you like.
Try to design other
stand-up animals.

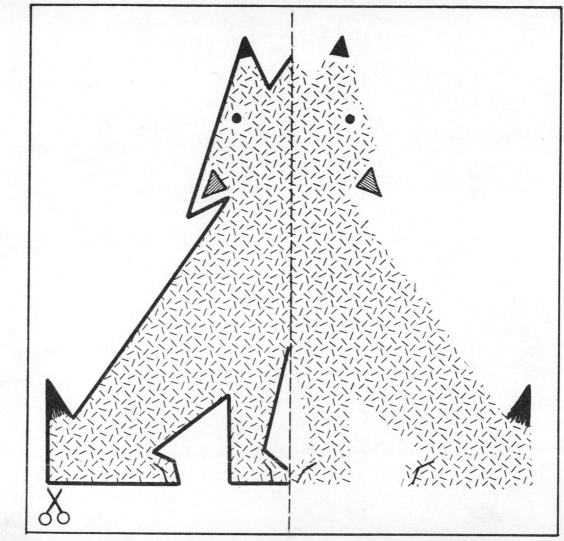

SANTA CLAUS

Cut out the square.
Cut away the
shaded area.
Color Santa Claus
any way you like.
Fold on the broken
lines to the BACK.
Spread the paper to
make Santa stand
up.

You can use Santa as a
table decoration or at-
tach a loop of thread
and hang him as a tree
ornament.

See back of page.

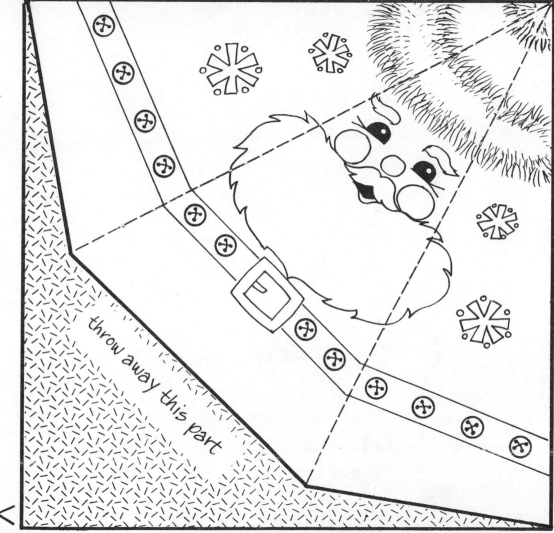

throw away this part

Suggestion

You can glue on cott
for Santa's beard and
fur.

MYSTERY OF THE PAPER CLIPS

For this trick you need two paper clips. When you perform the trick, the clips mysteriously hook together.

. Cut out the shaded rectangle.

. Fold to the BACK on the broken line; fold to you on the dotted line.

When you perform the trick:

. Slip on the paper clips like this: Place each paper clip over two layers of paper exactly as shown. Note that one side of each clip is inside a folded edge.

. Pull the ends of the paper apart. The paper clips will be hooked together. See back of page.

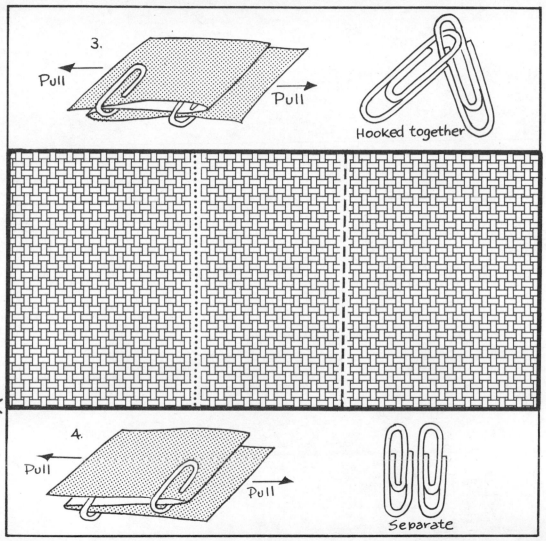

3.

Pull

Pull

Hooked together

4.

Pull

Pull

Separate

When you challenge a friend to repeat the trick:

5. Slip on the paper clips exactly as shown. Note that each paper clip is *around* a folded edge.
6. Hand the paper over to another person to pull the ends apart. The paper clips fall off separately.

Before you challenge your friends, practice both ways of putting the paper clips. Then you can do it quickly.

Suggestion

You can also work this trick with a dollar bill and two paper clips.

EARRINGS

1. Color the two rectangles any way you like. Cut them out on the solid lines.
2. Fan-pleat the paper by folding back and forth on the lines.
3. Wind a very narrow piece of sticky tape around one end of the fan. Spread open the other end.

See back of page.

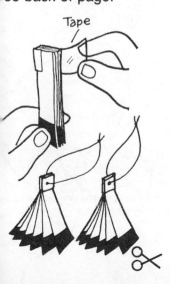

Tape

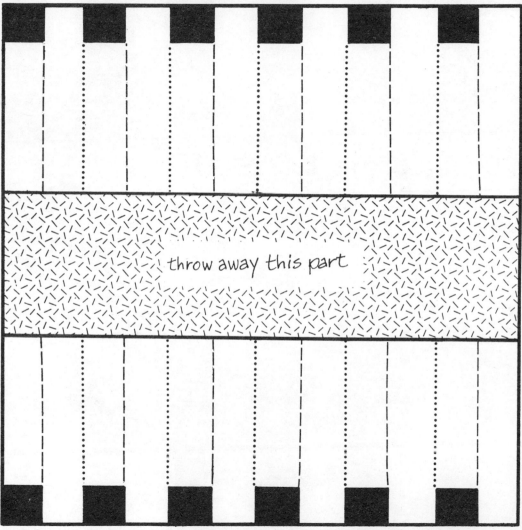

throw away this part

4. Thread a needle a[nd]
    pierce a hole at th[e]
    top of each earring[.]
    Leave enough
    thread to make lar[ge]
    loops to hang
    around your ears.

Suggestions

More earrings: Use g[ift]
wrap or other colored
paper. For each pair
two rectangles 5 inch[es]
by 2 inches (12 cm b[y]
cm).

WINDSURFER'S RACE

1. Cut out on the solid lines to make two surfboards and two sails.
2. Fold to the BACK on the broken lines.
3. Glue the sails on the boards with the tabs.

See back of page.

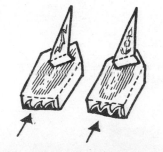

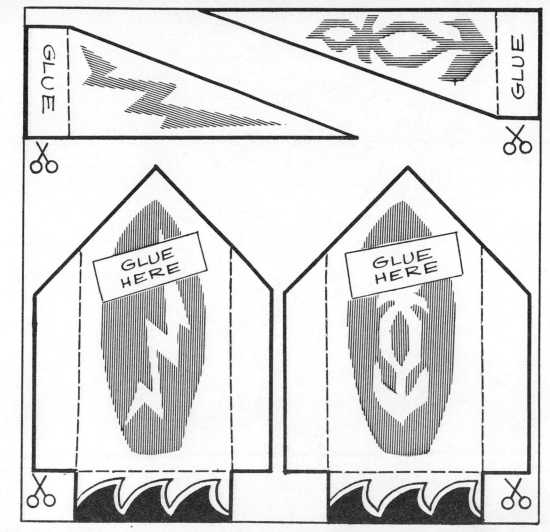

Rules of the game fo
two players:

Place the surfboards
a smooth table or a
desk. At an agreed
starting signal both
players blow on the
back of the windsurfe
The surfer who reach
the opposite side of t
table first is the winne

JUMPING MICE

1. Cut out the four squares. Fold each square in the same way.
2. Fold on the broken lines.
3. Overlap the black triangles and glue one on top of the other.
4. Tap the tail end of the mouse and it will do a backflip.

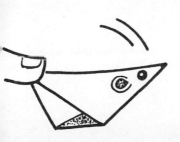

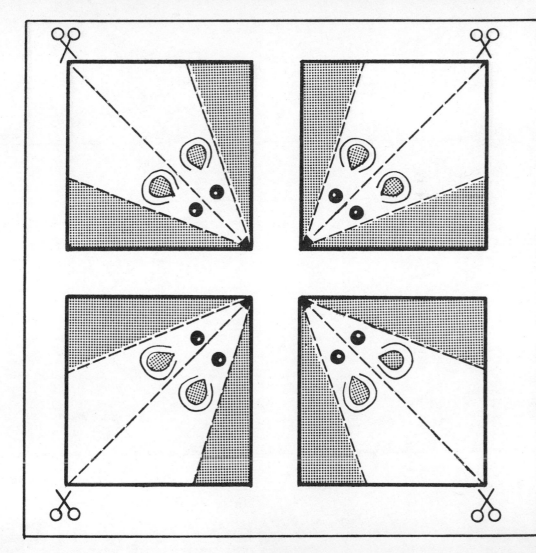

19

POP-UP VALENTINE

1. Cut out the rectangle. Fold it like a fan. Make sure the design shows on the outside of the folded fan.
2. Cut away the black parts through all layers of paper.
3. Cut a piece of red construction paper 8 inches × 5 inches. Fold it in half.
4. Glue the end panels of the fan inside the red paper. When you open the card the heart in the middle will pop up.

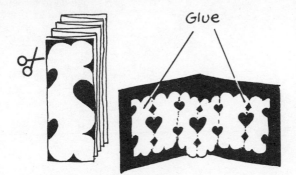

Glue

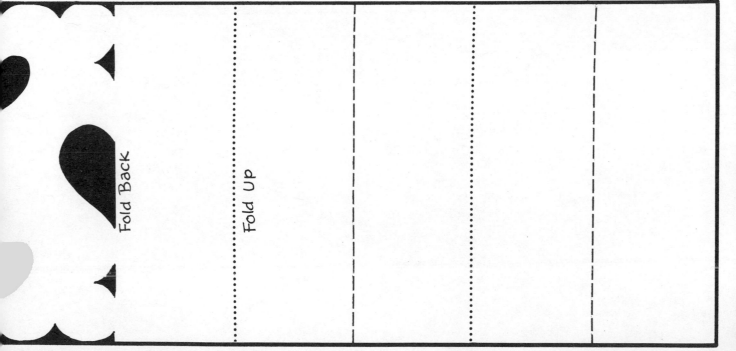

Fold Back

Fold Up

HI-FLYING AIRPLANE

1. Cut out the square of paper.
2. Fold the plane in half on the broken line to the BACK.
3. Cut out the plane on the solid line through both layers of paper.
4. Fold wings and rudders on the dotted lines to you.
5. Place a paper clip where shown.
6. Hold the plane underneath and throw it into the air slightly upward.

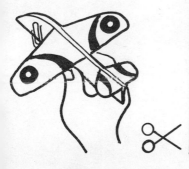

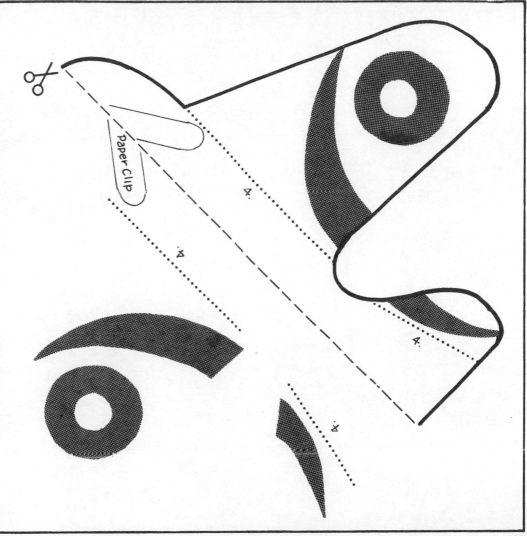

Paper Clip

THE BROKEN PLATE PUZZLE

Oh no! Tony broke a square plate by accident. He's found some special glue to repair it, but he can't fit the broken pieces together. Can you help him make a square with the four pieces?

1. Cut out the four pieces.
2. Arrange the four pieces into a square.

Another Puzzle:

When you have solved the Broken Plate Puzzle, try to arrange the same four pieces into a cross.

See back of page for the solutions. Do not peek until you have tried to solve the puzzles.

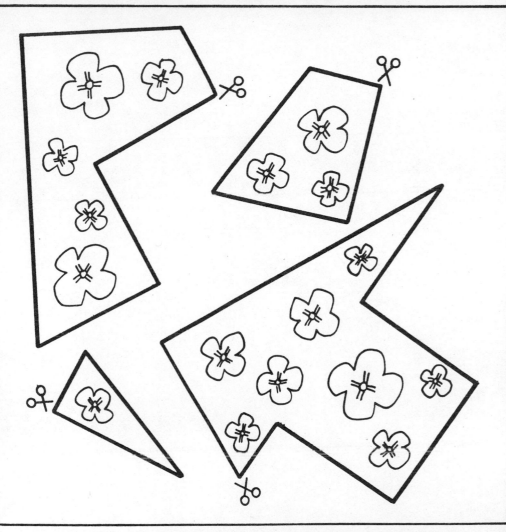

Solution for Broken Plate Puzzle:

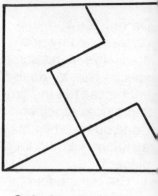

Solution for Cross Puzzle:

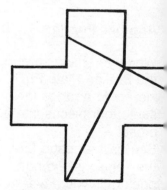

Now challenge your friends to make a square or a cross.

HEAVENLY ANGEL

1. Cut out the square.
2. Cut on the solid lines. The shaded parts fall off.
3. Fold the arms to the front on the dotted lines.
4. Slide slit A into slit B behind the angel.
5. Glue the hands together.

See back of page.

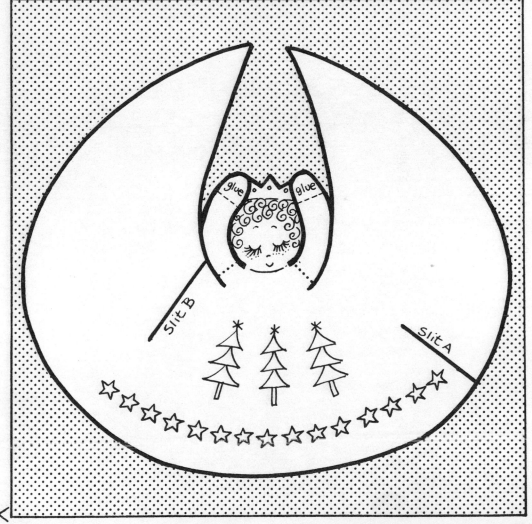

Suggestion

You can color the ang
and decorate it with g
ter or shiny stars.

DROOPY DOG

1. Cut out the square.
   Cut on the solid line
   from corner to cor-
   ner. Now, you have
   a triangle for the
   head and a triangle
   for the body.

Fold the head like this:

2. Fold to the BACK on
   line 1.
3. Fold to you on lines
   2, 3, and 4.
4. Fold to the BACK on
   line 5.

More instructions on
back of page.

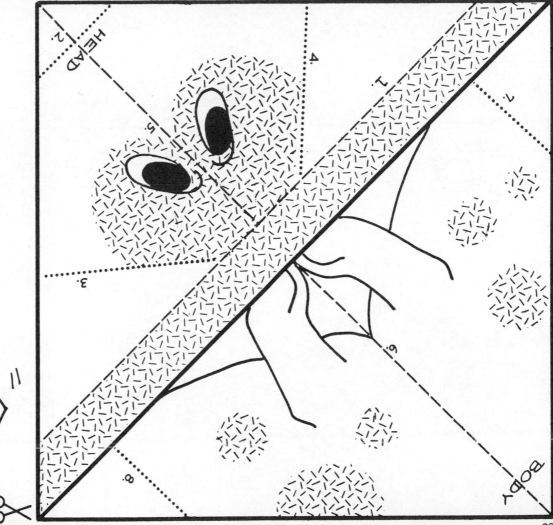

Fold the body like this

5. Fold to you on lines 6 and 7.

6. Fold to the BACK on line 8.

Put Droopy together like this:

7. Balance the head on the body. The edge of the folded-over piece at the back of the head rests on the corner. Give the head a little push and Droopy's head wiggles.

STARRY NIGHTS

It is very important that you look at the drawings and place your paper exactly as shown.

1. Cut out the shaded rectangles on this page.
2. Fold each rectangle in half on the dotted line.
3. Place both papers next to each other. Fold the outside corners down to the bottom edge.
4. Fold the other corners up to the top edge.
5. Fold both strips as shown on the dotted lines.

More instructions on next page.

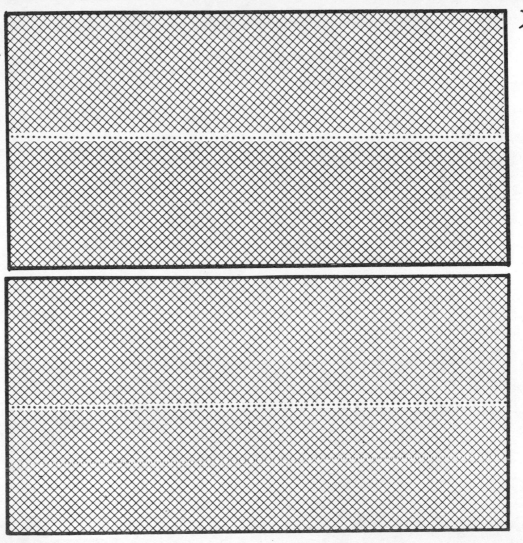

6a. Turn the front of this paper to the back, making the move from right t left.

6b. Swivel the other paper 90°.

7. Slide both papers top of each other See next drawing

8a. Fold the top corn DOWN and tuck it the "pocket" belo

8b. Fold the bottom corner UP and tud it in the "pocket" above.

9. Turn the star ove from right to left. Tuck the two big ners into the "po ets" as before.

10. Thread a string through a corner the star to hang

See next page.

You can make stars from foil-backed gift-wrap paper for holiday ornaments. Be sure the shiny side of the paper is on the outside after step 2.

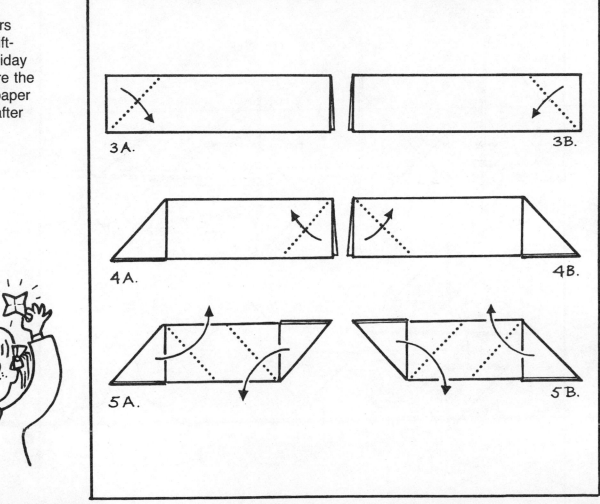

3A.

3B.

4A.

4B.

5A.

5B.

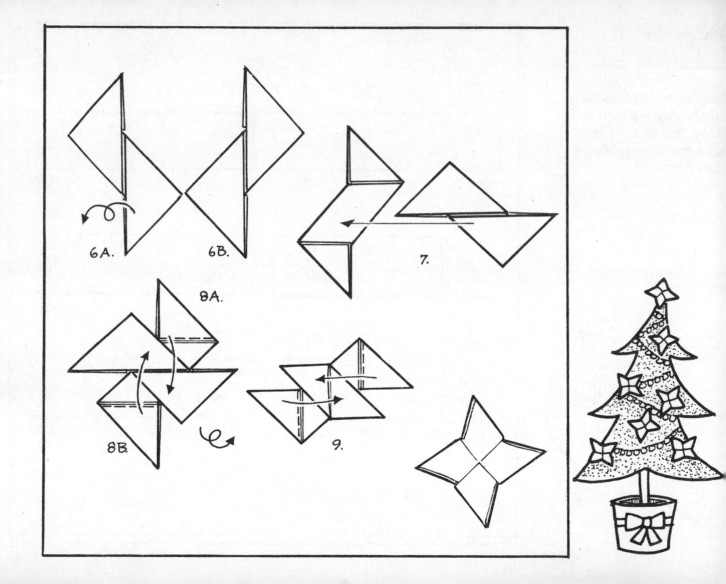

6A.

6B.

7.

8A.

8B.

9.

BEAUTIFUL BUTTERFLIES

1. Cut out the square. Cut from corner to corner on solid line 1. You have two triangles. Each triangle makes one butterfly.
2. Cut from the corner on the solid line 2.
3. Fold to the BACK on line 3.
4. Fold UP on lines 4 and 5.
5. Color your butterflies on the front and the back.
6. Hold the body of the butterfly with the wings on top. Move your hand up and down to flutter the butterfly's wings.

See back of page.

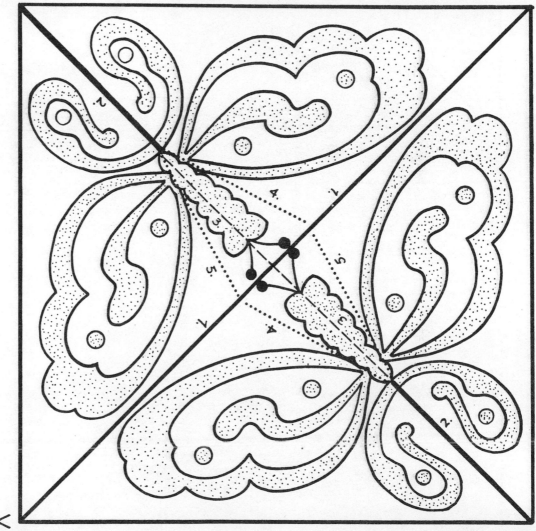

35

Suggestions

Greeting card: Glue a butterfly to a piece of stationery.

Hair ornament: Glue a butterfly to a hair bar-rette.

Table decorations: Make more butterflies and set them on the dinner table.

Mobile: Thread a loop through the body of a butterfly and hang it u

SPACE SHUTTLE

1. Cut out the square.
2. Fold to the BACK (mountain folds) on lines 1 to 7.
3. Fold UP (valley fold) on line 8.
4. Spread the wings. Place a piece of sticky tape on top of the plane near the nose. Hold the plane near the back and launch it in an upward path.

See back of page.

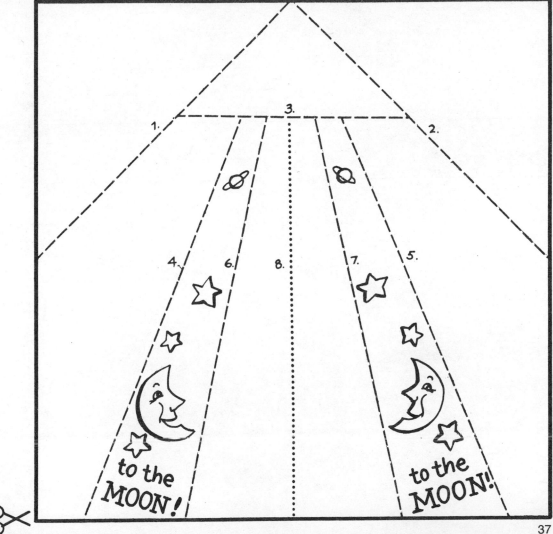

Suggestions

This is an excellent
flyer. You can experi-
ment to improve the
flight pattern:

 Sharpen all crease

 Change the launch
angle.

 Place a paper clip
the nose.

NINE-MAKES-TEN TRICK

Cut on the solid lines.
You have nine strips.
The trick is to make
nine strips into ten without cutting another strip.
Try it yourself before
looking at the solution
on the back of the
page. Then play the
trick on a friend.
See back of page for
the solution.

Solution for Nine-Makes-Ten Trick:

Arrange the nine strip to spell the word TEN

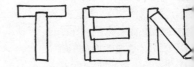

After you have played with the trick, you ca turn the strips into bir You need two strips make one bird.

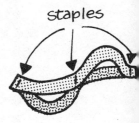

staples

FIGHTING TURTLES GAME

. Cut out the two tur-
  tles.
. Fold a pleat at the
  neck.
. Fold turtle in half to
  the BACK.
. Pull head up.
See back of page.

How to play the game—for one or t[wo] players:

Place both turtles fac[ing] each other, on a cere[al] or other kind of box. Tap on the box until one turtle falls off an[d] loses the game.

Other rules: Draw a [line] across the middle of [the] box. The turtle which crosses the line first [is] the winner. Invent m[ore] games.

ORIGAMI HOLIDAY ORNAMENT

Make very sharp creases all the time.

1. Cut out the square. Color the two ornaments and the two snowmen in any way you like.
2. Fold up on the diagonal dotted lines. Unfold paper flat again each time.
3. Fold to the BACK on the broken lines. Leave the paper folded in half on one of the broken lines.

More instructions on back of page.

43

4. Hold the paper exactly as shown. Push the sides together until your paper looks like a tent.
5. Your ornament is ready to hang with a loop of thread or a hook.

WINGED DINOSAUR

At each step make sure the paper looks exactly like the drawing and read the instructions out loud.

Cut out the square.

Fold UP on both diagonals (lines 1 and 2). Unfold paper after each crease.

Fold paper in half to the BACK on line 3. Unfold paper.

Fold paper in half to the BACK on line 4. Leave paper folded.

More instructions on next page.

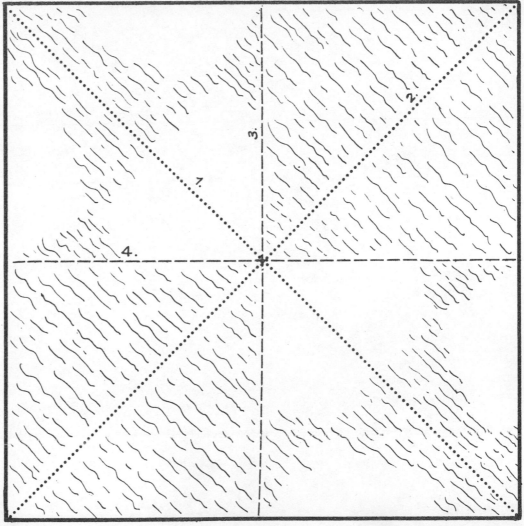

5. Grasp paper at th
   folded edge with
   both hands in the
   exact places show
   in the drawing. M
   your hands to eac
   other until the pap
   forms a square.
   Place it down flat.
   Make sure you ha
   two flaps on each
   side. If you have
   flap on one side a
   three on the other
   flip one flap over.
6. Place closed corn
   of the square awa
   from you. Fold the
   outer edges on th
   front flaps to the
   middle crease. Tu
   the paper over an
   repeat this with th
   two flaps on the
   back.
7. Fold the triangle a
   the top back and
   forth. The paper
   looks the same as
   before but the
   crease made on t

dotted line helps you with the next step.

a. Open the front flaps slightly. Find the loose corner at the bottom and lift it up in the direction of the arrow until you see the crease you made in step 7.

b. Move the outside edges of the paper to the middle and flatten it into a long diamond. Turn the paper over and repeat step 8 on the back.

9. Fold the flap over from right to left, like you turn the page of a book. Turn the paper over and repeat this on the back, again folding from right to left.

More instructions back of page.

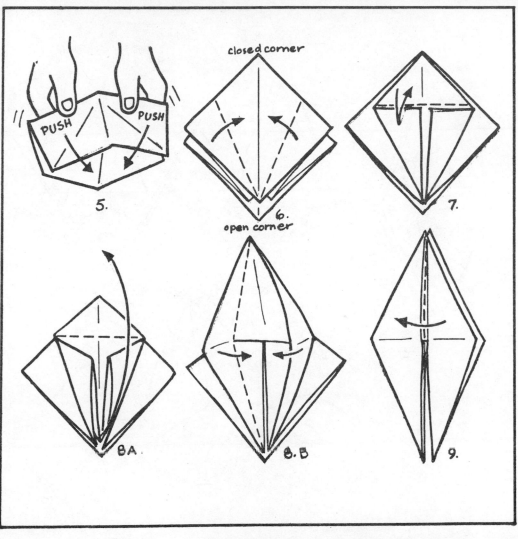

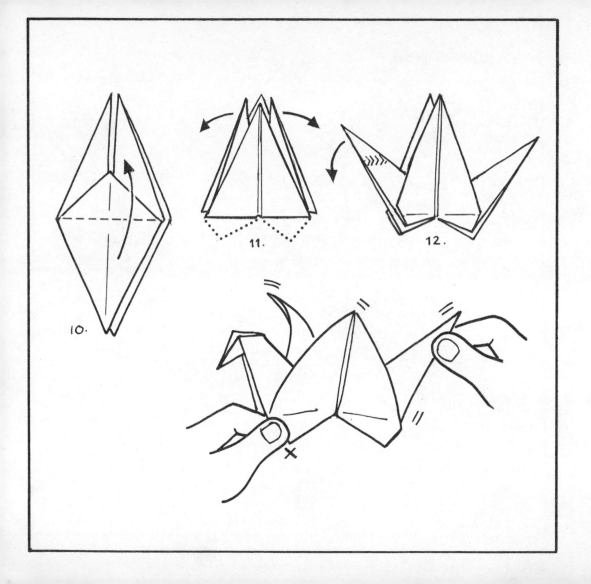

10. Fold the bottom flap up as far as will go. Turn the paper over and r[e]peat on the back.

11. Pull the hidden points in the dire[c]tion of the arrow[s] one at a time. T[o] make them stay, crease sharply a[s] shown by the dotted lines.

12. Fold the head d[own] in between the t[wo] layers of the nec[k]. You have now folded your ptero[] dactyl. It will flap [its] wings if you hold [it] at X with one ha[nd] and gently pull th[e] tail back and fort[h] with the other ha[nd]. Do not pull the ta[il] up and down.

Hint: If the wings don[t] flap, then reach insid[e] tween a wing and the[] and wiggle the wing. Do this on both sides